2

Congratulations! You are holding in your hands one of the most effective tools for test preparation available. The effectiveness of flashcards joined with the convenience and ease of use of a book. We want to offer a quick reminder about how these flashcards are set up and what you can expect.

As you will see, there are two "sets" of flashcards. The top set has a grey background. The bottom set has plain white background. In either case, the question is on the right page and you simply flip the page to see the answer, just like with a traditional flashcard. We highly suggest working through one set at time.

As you will notice, there are different types of questions on the flashcards. None are intended to necessarily be "harder" or "easier", but instead intended to challenge you in different ways. Some have multiple choice questions, which will allow you to think critically as well as get practice for the style of questions you will encounter on the exam. Other flash cards however will provide no clues! This will require you to mentally recall information on your own without the benefit of seeing possible answer choices.

The goal is to engage your brain in different ways so that your studying time is as effective as possible and you retain the necessary information for the test. Unlike with rote memorization or simply reading from a book, you will not experience brain-drain and lose information because you mind is actively engaged the entire time. Less studying, but greater retention of information!

With that, let's get started on the next page. Simply read the question and flip the page to see if you got it right. Remember, work across the entire top (grey) set first, then come back to page 1 and start the bottom (white) set.

Good luck, and again congratulations on your upcoming fantastic test score!

The integument (skin) makes up what percent of the body's overall weight?
- A. 5%
- B. 12%
- C. 18%
- D. 22%

Which type of hearing loss is caused by a lesion of the cochlea or neural path that results in a defect in receptors or the vestibulocochlear nerve?

Answer: C. 18%

Explanation: The integument is the skin, which makes up around 18% of the body's weight.

Sensorineural hearing loss

What is the function of the skin?
- A. Regulate body temperature
- B. Manufacture vitamins
- C. Protect from microorganisms
- D. All of the above

A hordelolum is also called:

Answer: D. All of the above
Explanation: Skin is necessary to protect a person form the invasion of microorganisms, as well as to regulate body temperature and manufacture vitamins.

A stye

The outermost layer of skin is:
  A. Epidermis
  B. Dermis
  C. Hypodermis
  D. Subcutaneous

What is volume 1 of the *International Classification of Diseases* (ICD) Ninth Revision (9) Clinical Modifications (CM) manual (ICD-9-CM) called?

Answer: A. Epidermis

Explanation: The epidermis is the outermost layer, and it contains four sections called stratum. The stratum basale is the deepest section. The second skin layer is the dermis, which contains two sections: papillare and reticulare. Also in the dermis are nerves, blood vessels, nails, glands, hair, and connective tissue. The subcutaneous tissue is also called the hypodermis, which contains connective tissue and fat tissue and connects the skin to underlying muscle.

Diseases, Tabular

The sebaceous glands are in the:
- A. Epidermis
- B. Dermis
- C. Hypodermis
- D. Subcutaneous

Which ICD-9 convention is used to enclose synonyms, explanatory phrases, and alternative wording?

Answer: B. Dermis

Explanation: The sebaceous (oil) glands are in the dermis, and they secrete oil (sebum) that lubricates the skin and hair. The sudoriferous (sweat) glands are also in the dermis, and they secrete salty water to cool the body.

Brackets

Anhidrosis is:
  A. Too much of or increased sweat
  B. Lack of or decreased sweat
  C. Too much of or increased oil
  D. Lack of or decreased oil

What ICD-9 codes are used to provide additional information regarding the exact nature of injury or poisoning?

Answer: B. Lack of or decreased sweat
Explanation: Hyperhydrosis is too much or increased sweat, and anhidrosis is lack of or decreased sweat.

E codes

Which of the following is a fatty tissue tumor?
   A. Adipose
   B. Hematoma
   C. Lipoma
   D. Steatoma

What is the purpose of an inclusion note?

Answer: C. Lipoma

Explanation: Adipose tissue is another name for fat tissue. A hematoma is a localized collection of blood. A steatoma is a fatty mass of the sebaceous gland. A lipoma is a simple, fatty mass of the skin.

To further define or give examples of the content.

Which type of dermatitis is common in young children?

    A. Atopic
    B. Contact
    C. Stasis
    D. Seborrheic

Which of the following is NOT one of the organizations who developed the ICD-9-CM coding guidelines?

Answer: A. Atopic

Explanation: Atopic dermatitis (eczema) is caused by irritants or allergens that activate mast cells, eosinophils, T lymphocytes, and monocytes. It occurs in those with a family history of the condition, as well as asthma and allergies, and it is more common in infants and children.

American Medical Association (AMA)

An irregular-shaped, elevated scar that occurs from excessive collagen in the corneum during tissue repair is:

A. Macule
B. Papule
C. Keloid
D. Nodule

Codes that describe the signs and symptoms rather than a diagnosis are only first-listed when:

Answer: C. Keloid

Explanation: A macule is a flat skin mole or freckle. A papule is a solid, elevated 1.0 cm skin lesion, such as a wart, mole, or lichen planus. A nodule is a solid, elevated 1- 2 cm skin lesion , such as a lipoma, lymph node, erythema nodusoum. A keloid is an irregular-shaped, elevated scar that occurs from excessive collagen in the corneum during tissue repair.

No diagnosis is established or confirmed by a physician.

A fissure is:
A. Skin cracks, such as athlete's foot or cracks in the corners of the mouth
B. Loss of a portion of the skin, which is a physiologic response to aging
C. Temporary, localized skin elevation, such as an insect bite or allergic reaction
D. Dried skin exudate (scab)

When can chronic condition codes be used?

Answer: A. Skin cracks, such as athlete's foot or cracks in the corners of the mouth

Explanation: A wheal is temporary, localized skin elevation, such as an insect bite or allergic reaction. Atrophy is loss of a portion of the skin, which is a physiologic response to aging. A crust is dried skin exudate (scab).

As long as the patient is receiving care for that diagnosis

Which of the following skin conditions is associated with a herald patch?
- A. Stasis dermatitis
- B. Psoriasis
- C. Pityriasis rosea
- D. None of the above

If routine testing is performed during the same encounter to evaluate a sign, symptom, or diagnosis, the coder should:

Answer: C. Pityriasis rosea

Explanation: Stasis dermatitis is associated with phlebitis, varicosities, and vascular trauma, and it begins with pruritus and erythema and progresses to hyperpigmentation, scaling, petechia, and ulcerated lesions. The cause of psoriasis is unknown, but thought to be caused from immunologic disorder, a triggering agent, or biochemical alterations. It results in well-demarcated plaques and scaly, flaky, and inflamed skin. The cause of pityriasis is unknown, but it is associated with a primary lesion is called "herald patch," which is a salmon-colored, circular 3 to 4 cm lesion. Secondary lesions are oval, reddened, and itchy, occurring around days 14 to 21.

Assign the V code first, followed by a secondary code describing the reason for the non-routine test.

Which skin tumor is benign?
  A. Melanoma
  B. Kaposi's sarcoma
  C. Keratoacanthoma
  D. Basal cell carcinoma

For a patient who is receiving chemotherapy, radiation therapy, or rehabilitation, the coder should:

Answer: C. Keratoacanthoma

Explanation: Three common benign skin tumors are seborrheic keratosis, actinic keratosis, and keratoacanthoma, which is a scaly pigmented patch that occurs in hair follicles. Basal cell carcinoma is a shiny, reddened cancerous lesion that is slow growing in deep skin layers and basal cells. Melanoma is a malignant lesion that originates in the melanocytes. Kaposi's sarcoma is a rare form of vascular skin cancer that is associated with HIV/AIDS.

Use an appropriate V code first, followed by a secondary code for the diagnosis or problem that requires treatment.

Which infection that results due to injury and is caused by Staphylococcus?
   A. Cellulitis
   B. Folliculitis
   C. Furuncle
   D. Impetigo

When an episode of healthcare involves a number of related conditions, and when no one condition predominates, the coder should:

Answer: A. Cellulitis

Explanation: Folliculitis is an infection of the hair follicles that results in erythema and pustules. A furuncle is a boil caused by an infected hair follicle. Impetigo is a highly contagious pyoderma caused by Staphylococcus.

Use a code that incorporates multiple conditions as the "main" code.

This infection is caused by the herpes virus:
 A. Cold sores of the mouth
 B. Genital sores
 C. Shingles
 D. All of the above

A 36 year old man has returned for his HIV test results, and he was recently found to be HIV positive. What should the coder use for this encounter?

Answer: D. All of the above

Explanation: Herpes simplex virus (HSV) (cold sores) are red blisters near the lips and mouth (type 1 HSV-1) or genital area (type 2 HSV-2). Herpes zoster (shingles) is red blisters that burn and sting and occur on an area of skin innervated by one of the cranial nerves.

V65.44 HIV counseling

Which form of tinea occurs on the feet?
- A. Manis
- B. Capitus
- C. Corporis
- D. Pedis

When coding for a neoplasm, what should the coder do first:

Answer: D. Pedis
Explanation: Tinea capitis occurs on the scalp. Tinea corporis (ringworm) can occur anywhere on the body. Tinea manis occurs on the hands. Tinea unguium occurs on the nails. Tinea pedis occurs on the feet.

Go to the Neoplasm Table in the Alphabetic Index.

Which of the following is NOT a symptom of acne vulgaris?
  A. Blackheads
  B. Pustules
  C. Macules
  D. Papules

When therapy is given to a patient with cancer, the coder should:

Answer: C. Macules

Explanation: The symptoms of acne vulgaris include blackheads, whiteheads, pustules, cysts, and papules.

First code for the treatment, followed by a secondary neoplasm code.

How many bones are in the human body?
   A. 100
   B. 106
   C. 200
   D. 206

A patient with bone cancer is having a reduction procedure for a broken radius (right arm). What should be coded first?

Answer: D. 206
Explanation: The musculoskeletal system is comprised of the bony skeleton, skeletal muscles, cardiac muscles, and smooth muscles. There also are 206 bones, as well as cartilage and ligaments. The muscular system protects the organs, produces heat, assists with movement, and forms body shape.

The fracture

Which of the following is NOT considered to be a long bone?
  A. Femur
  B. Scapula
  C. Tibia
  D. Humerus

For a patient with extensive metastasis where the physician is unable to determine the site of primary malignancy, what code should be used?

Answer: B. Scapula

Explanation: The long bones are tubular bones, including the femur, tibia, fibula, humerus, ulna, radius bones. The short bones are cuboidal bones, such as the carpals and tarsals. The flat bones are thin and flat, such as the skull, sternum, and scapula. Seasamoid bones are rounded, such as the patella. The zygoma and vertebra are irregular bones.

Malignant neoplasm, unspecified

Which of the following is NOT one of the middle ear bones?
    A. Malleus
    B. Ethmoid
    C. Incus
    D. Stapes

When it is documented that the patient uses insulin, but the type of diabetes is not recorded, the coder should use:

Answer: B. Ethmoid

Explanation: The axial skeleton includes the skull, hyoid bone, vertebral column, sacrum, ribs, and sternum. The skull bones include the frontal (forehead), parietal (sides), temporal (lower sides), occipital (posterior), sphenoid (floor), ethmoid (between eye orbits and nasal cavity) styloid process (below ear), and zygomatic process (cheek). The middle ear bones include the malleus (hammer), incus (anvil), and stapes (stirrup).

A code for Type 2 diabetes mellitus, followed by a secondary code for Long-term use of insulin.

Which facial bone is the cheekbone?
  A. Maxilla
  B. Nasal
  C. Zygomatic
  D. Vomer

If the type of diabetes mellitus is not documented in the medical record the default diagnosis is:

Answer: C. Zygomatic

Explanation: The facial bones include the maxilla (upper jaw), nasal (bridge of nose), zygomatic (cheekbone), mandible (jaw), lacrimal (near eye orbits), vomer (nasal septum), palate (between oral and nasal cavities), and nasal conchae (turbinates).

Type II diabetes

What is the upper portion of the pelvis called?
  A. Pubis symphysis
  B. Ischium
  C. Pubis
  D. Ilium

For an encounter due to an insulin pump malfunction resulting in an overdose of insulin, the coder should:

Answer: D. Ilium

Explanation: The pelvis contains the ilium (upper part), ischium (posterior part), pubis (anterior part), and pubis symphysis (cartilage of the pubic bones).

Use code 996.57, Mechanical complication due to insulin pump, as the principal code for an encounter due to an insulin pump malfunction resulting in an overdose of insulin, followed by code 962.3, Poisoning by insulin.

This bone is the smaller of the two lower arm bones?

      A. Radius
      B. Ulna
      C. Humerus
      D. Talus

For aplastic anemia that is drug-induced or due to other external causes, the coder should:

Answer: B. Ulna

Explanation: The two lower arm bones are the radius (larger) and ulna (smaller). The humerus is the upper arm bone, and the talus is the ankle bone.

Use first a code to identify the substance, followed by the anemia code.

Which type of tissue lines the bowel, blood vessels, and urethra?
    A. Visceral
    B. Skeletal
    C. Cardiac
    D. None of the above

Subcategory 285.2, Anemia in chronic illness, has codes that may be used as secondary codes if treatment of the anemia is:

Answer: A. Visceral

Explanation: Skeletal tissue is the striated tissue that attaches to bones. Cardiac tissue is heart muscle that is both striated and smooth. Visceral tissue is smooth tissue that lines the bowel, blood vessels, and urethra.

Not the primary reason for the encounter, but is included in the visit.

Which of the following muscles is not matched with the appropriate action?

A. Trapezius – Extends head
B. Deltoid – Abducts upper arm
C. Sternocleidomastoid – Grates teeth
D. Pectoralis major – Flexes upper arm

Codes in chapter 5 include personality disorders, neuroses, psychoses, stress disorders, and sexual deviation conditions, and the fifth digit represents all of the following statuses EXCEPT:

Answer: C. Sternocleidomastoid – Grates teeth
Explanation: The pterygolds muscle grates the teeth, and the sternocleidomastoid muscle flexes the head. Choices A, B, and C are matched correctly.

3 – chronic

Which of the following pertains to cartilage?
A. Chondral
B. Ganglion
C. Articular
D. Bursa

If delirium is due to a known physiological condition, the coder should:

Answer: A. Chondral
Explanation: Chondral pertains to cartilage. A ganglion is a knot-like cyst. Articular pertains to a joint, and a bursa is a joint sac.

First code for the underlying condition, followed by a secondary code for Delirium due to known physiological condition.

This injury is a compound break where the bone penetrates the skin:

- A. Complete fracture
- B. Incomplete fracture
- C. Open fracture
- D. Closed fracture

Avoid the use of the code for central pain syndrome and chronic pain syndrome unless:

Answer: C. Open fracture

Explanation: A closed fracture is a simple break where the bone does not penetrate the skin. A complete fracture is a break where the bone is in two pieces or more (oblique, spiral, linear, and transverse). An incomplete fracture is a break where the bone is not broken in two or more pieces (greenstick, torus, stress, and bowing).

The provider has specifically documented this as a diagnosis.

What causes osteomyelitis?
- A. Advancing age
- B. Bacteria
- C. Viruses
- D. Decreased bone mass

If the pain is not specified as acute or chronic, avoid use of codes from category 338, except for:

Answer: B. Bacteria

Explanation: Osteomyelitis is a bone infection caused by bacteria. Osteoporosis is decreased bone mass and density that occurs due to malabsorption of calcium and other substances and is associated with advancing age. Osteomalacia is softening of adult bones.

Post-thoracotomy pain, postoperative pain, and neoplasm-related pain

This joint disorder is caused by excessive uric acid:

   A. Spina bifida
   B. Septic arthritis
   C. Gouty arthritis
   D. Ankylosing spondylosis

A patient is being treated for pain, which is related to a neoplasm. She is not receiving treatment for the neoplasm during this visit. The physician lists "Pain secondary to malignancy," but he does not specify whether the pain is acute or chronic. What should the coder use as the first listed code?

Answer: C. Gouty arthritis

Explanation: Spina bifida is a congenital abnormality where vertebrae do not close around the spinal cord. Septic arthritis is an infectious process that generally affects a single joint. Ankylosing spondylosis is a progressive inflammatory disease that affects vertebral joints. Gouty arthritis is a joint condition caused by uric acid accumulation.

Code 338.3

Which condition has a genetic predisposition?
   A. Polymyositis
   B. Fibromylagia
   C. Muscular dystrophy
   D. All of the above

Where is the hypertension table located in the ICD-9-CM manual?

Answer: C. Muscular dystrophy

Explanation: Muscular dystrophy is a progressive degenerative muscle disorder that has a genetic predisposition. Fibromyalgia is a condition that involves generalized pain and aching that often affects middle-aged women. Polymyositis is generalized muscle inflammation that causes weakness.

The Alphabetic Index under "H"

Which bone tumor is usually benign?
- A. Chondroblastoma
- B. Multiple myeloma
- C. Rhabdomyosarcoma
- D. Osteosarcoma

A patient has hypertensive chronic kidney disease, and is seen for this problem. The physician lists the condition as stage 3. What should the coder do?

Answer: A. Chondroblastoma
Explanation: Both chondroblastoma and osteoma are benign. Multiple myeloma is malignant cells in the soft tissue and skeleton. Rhabdomyosarcoma is an aggressive and invasive malignant carcinoma. Osteosarcoma is a malignant tumor of the long bones.

Code from the subcategory 403 and assign a fifth digit of 0.

Which type of arthritis is considered to be an autoimmune disease?
- A. Osteoarthritis
- B. Rheumatoid arthritis
- C. Septic arthritis
- D. Gouty arthritis

A patient suffered a cerebrovascular event, but did not acquire any neurologic deficits. How would this be coded?

Answer: B. Rheumatoid arthritis

Explanation: Osteoarthritis is degeneration and inflammation of the joint.

Rheumatoid arthritis is progressive autoimmune disease that affects the connective tissues and joints. Septic arthritis is an infectious process that generally affects a single joint. Gouty arthritis is caused by excessive uric acid in the joints.

With a code for transient ischemic attack, followed by code for cerebral infarction without residual deficits.

Which of the following is NOT part of the lower respiratory tract?
- A. Turbinates
- B. Bronchial tree
- C. Trachea
- D. Lungs

A patient has peritonsillar abscess caused by Streptococcus. How would this be coded?

Answer: A. Turbinates

Explanation: The upper respiratory tract includes the nose, sinuses, turbinates, pharynx, and larynx. The lower respiratory tract involves the trachea, bronchial tree, and lungs. Both upper and lower structures supply oxygen and rid the body of carbon dioxide.

First-listed code for peritonsillar abscess, followed by a secondary code for the infectious agent.

Which structure is considered the voicebox?
   A. Pharynx
   B. Larynx
   C. Turbinates
   D. Conchae

When coding a chronic condition for a patient who
has a history of smoking, the coder would:

Answer: B. Larynx

Explanation: The turbinates are also called conchae, and they are the bones of the nose that are inferior, middle, or superior. The pharynx is the throat passageway for air and food. The larynx is the voicebox that contains vocal cords and cartilage.

First assign a code for the lung condition, followed by a secondary code for personal history of nicotine dependence.

When the skin or lips are bluish, this is called:
  A. Asphyxia
  B. Cyanosis
  C. Orthopnea
  D. Tachypnea

A patient is admitted with a respiratory condition related to HIV infection. The patient doesn't want his insurance to know about his HIV status. What should the coder do?

Answer: B. Cyanosis

Explanation: Asphyxia is lack of oxygen, orthopnea is shortness of breath with lying, and tachypnea is rapid respirations. When the skin and/or lips get blue, this is called cyanosis.

Explain to the patient that the HIV must be reported, and code the HIV disease first, followed by the code for the respiratory condition.

The physician has documented nose bleed in the medical record. To code this visit, what would you search for in the Alphabetic Index?

A. Atelectasis
B. Epitaxis
C. Cyanosis
D. Pleuritis

A patient with gingivitis has documented history of chewing tobacco use. The physician only lists "gingivitis" as the diagnosis. What should the coder do?

Answer: B. Epitaxis
Explanation: The medical term for nose bleed is epitaxis. Atelectasis is incomplete lung expansion, cyanosis is bluish discoloration of the skin and lips, and pleuritis is inflammation of the pleura.

Code first for the gingivitis, followed by a secondary code for history of tobacco use or tobacco use.

The patient has documented symptoms of hemoptysis and rhinorrhea and no existing diagnosis. What do these terms mean?

A. The patient is coughing up blood up blood and has drainage from the nose.
B. The patient is coughing up sputum and has blood draining from the nose.
C. The patient has lung and nose pain.
D. None of the above.

A patient comes in for stress incontinence. She has a long-standing history of a neurogenic bladder, COPD, and hypertension, but this is the first mention of incontinence. The physician lists only a diagnosis of stress incontinence for this encounter, and he does not treat any existing chronic conditions. How would this visit be coded?

Answer: A. The patient is coughing up blood up blood and has drainage from the nose
Explanation: Hemoptysis is coughing up blood, and rhinorrhea is drainage from the nose.

The first-listed code would be Neuromuscular dysfunction of bladder, followed by a secondary code for Stress incontinence.

What condition is acute injury to the alveolocapillary membrane, which results in atelectasis and edema?

A. Acute respiratory failure
B. Respiratory acidosis
C. Pneumothorax
D. Adult respiratory distress syndrome

In Chapter 11, Complications of Pregnancy, Childbirth, and the Puerperium, the fifth digit denotes which episodes of care?

Answer: D. Adult respiratory distress syndrome
Explanation: Acute respiratory failure is a condition of inadequate gas exchange that results in hypoxemia. Respiratory acidosis is excess retention of carbon dioxide leads to low level of pH. A pneumothorax is a condition where air collects in the pleural cavity.

Adult Respiratory Distress Syndrome (ARDS) is an acute injury to the alveolocapillary membrane that results in atelectasis and edema.

1 – delivered, with or without antepartum condition; 2 – delivered with mention of postpartum complication; and 3 – antepartum condition/complication

The chronic dilation of the bronchi associated with bronchiectasis can be:
  A. Cylindrical
  B. Varicose
  C. Cystic
  D. All of the above

When a pregnant woman has an injury or illness that is unrelated to her pregnancy, the coder should:

Answer: D. All of the above

Explanation: With bronchiectasis, the chronic dilation of the bronchi can be cylindrical, varicose, cystic, or sacular.

Code first for the illness or injury, followed by the secondary code V22.2, Pregnant state incidental.

Which of the following is not a substance that lodges in a pulmonary artery and causes a pulmonary embolism?

    A. Air
    B. Blood clot
    C. Tissue
    D. Pus

If an abortion is documented as "incomplete," what fifth digit would be added to the abortion code?

Answer: D. Pus
Explanation: A pulmonary embolism is caused by occlusion due to air, blood clot, or tissue that lodges in a pulmonary artery.

1

With an empyema, there is pus in:
  A. The pleural space
  B. The pulmonary artery
  C. The bronchioles
  D. The lung tissue

A pregnant woman, who has had type 1 diabetes since age 7, is pregnant. She is being seen in the prenatal clinic. How would the coder document this?

Answer: A. The pleural space
Explanation: Empyema is infectious pleura effusion where there is pus in the pleural space.

With code 648.0x, Diabetes mellitus complicating pregnancy, followed by a secondary code from category 250, Diabetes mellitus.

Which of the following is NOT a form of COPD?
   A. Chronic bronchitis
   B. Emphysema
   C. Pneumonia
   D. All of the above are forms of COPD

For coding skin change changes from exposure to radiation, the coder should:

Answer: C. Pneumonia

Explanation: Pneumonia is an acute condition where there is inflammation of the lungs due to aspiration, bacteria, protozoa, viruses, fungi, or chlamydia. Chronic Obstructive Pulmonary Disease (COPD) is a chronic, irreversible obstruction of the lungs that decreases expiration. Chronic bronchitis is a form of COPD that causes dyspnea, wheezing, and productive cough. Emphysema is another form of COPD that causes enlargement of alveoli and loss of lung elasticity.

First list a code for the ultraviolet radiation, followed by a code for the type of skin condition.

When there is increased carbon dioxide in the arterial blood caused by poor alveoli ventilation, the condition is called:

A. Hypoxemia
B. Hypercapnia
C. Bronchiectasis
D. Bronchiolitis

A patient has a foreign body of the soft muscle tissue of the lower left leg. The physician only treats him to remove this object. How would this be coded?

Answer: B. Hypercapnia

Explanation: Hypercapnia is increased carbon dioxide in the arterial blood caused by poor alveoli ventilation. Hypoxemia is reduced oxygenation of the arterial blood. Bronchiectasis is chronic dilation of the bronchi that can be cylindrical, varicose, cystic, or sacular. Bronchiolitis is obstruction of the bronchioles caused by inflammation from a viral pathogen, such as RSV.

With a first-listed code for Foreign body of the soft muscle tissue, followed by a secondary code for the type of foreign body.

With respiratory acidosis, what happens to the pH level?
   A. It goes up.
   B. It goes down.
   C. It stays the same.
   D. It fluctuates.

A newborn infant is liveborn with a congenital anomaly and was born prematurely. How would this be coded?

Answer: B. It goes down.
Explanation: With respiratory acidosis, there is excess retention of carbon dioxide, which leads to a low level of pH.

With a first-listed code for Liveborn, followed by secondary codes for Low birth weight and immaturity status and a code to document the anomaly.

With pneumoconiosis, particles invade the lung tissue, such as:
- A. Blood clots, air, or cholesterol
- B. Pus, fluid, and WBCs
- C. Coal, asbestos, or fiberglass
- D. All of the above

A patient was started on an antihistamine for allergies one week ago. Today, she is in the office for urinary retention. The physician's diagnosis is "Urinary retention, secondary to medication." How would this be coded?

Answer: C. Coal, asbestos, or fiberglass
Explanation: With pneumoconiosis, coal, asbestos, or fiberglass particles invade the tissue.

First list a code to identify the drug, followed by a secondary code for urinary retention.

What lung condition is often caused by an upper respiratory infection?
   A. Pneumoconiosis
   B. Pulmonary embolism
   C. Pleurisy
   D. COPD

A patient received numerous second-degree burns to the face and hands, and one small first-degree burn to the left thigh. How would this be coded?

Answer: C. Pleurisy

Explanation: Pneumoconiosis is caused by particles in the lung tissue. Pulmonary embolism (PE) is caused by occlusion due to air, blood clot, or tissue that lodges in a pulmonary artery. COPD is caused by smoking. Pleurisy, also called pleuritis, is inflammation of the pleura due to an upper respiratory infection.

First list a code for the first-degree burn, followed by secondary codes for the second-degree burns.

What is the function of the respiratory tract?
    A. Supply the body with oxygen
    B. Rid the body of carbon dioxide
    C. Both A and B
    D. Neither A nor B

A patient has overdosed on Valium, but he survived the incident. He has a long-standing history of benzodiazepine abuse. How would this be coded?

Answer: C. Both A and B

Explanation: The upper respiratory tract includes the nose, sinuses, turbinates, pharynx, and larynx. The lower respiratory tract involves the trachea, bronchial tree, and lungs. All of these structures supply oxygen and rid the body of carbon dioxide.

Code first with the poisoning code, followed by a secondary code for the overdose and an additional code for drug abuse or dependence to the substance.

What component of the cardiovascular system transports nutrients and hormones?
A. The heart
B. The blood
C. The vessels
D. All of the above

True or False: The Supplementary Classification of Factors Influencing Health Status and Contact with Health Services (V01.0 - V91.99) involves the following circumstances for the use of V codes: A person encounters the health services to act as an organ donor, to receive inoculations or health screenings, or to receive counseling; issues or problems influence a person's health status but do not involve a current illness or injury; and a person who has a resolved or resolving condition must use health services for aftercare.

Answer: B. The blood

Explanation: The cardiovascular system consists of the heart, blood, and blood vessels. The vessels carry blood throughout the body, the heart pumps the blood and allows for oxygen-carbon dioxide exchange, and the blood transports nutrients and hormones.

True

What percentage of water is plasma?
- A. 9%
- B. 19%
- C. 91%
- D. 99%

_____ Codes are status codes that are used when a patient is a carrier of a disease, when a patient has the sequelae of a past condition, and for the presence of a mechanical device.

Answer: C. 91%
Explanation: Plasma is the liquid part of the blood that is 91% water.

V

All of the following are part of cellular blood EXCEPT:

A. Plasma
B. Leukocytes
C. Thrombocytes
D. Erythrocytes

When is it appropriate to use code V45.88, Do not resuscitate status?

Answer: A. Plasma
Explanation: The liquid part of the blood is called plasma (mostly water), and the cellular part contains leukocytes (white blood cells or WBCs), erythrocytes (red blood cells or RBCs), and thrombocytes (platelets).

When it is documented by the provider

The vessels that lead away from the heart are the:
   A. Veins
   B. Arteries
   C. Capillaries
   D. Venules

What code would be used for a patient who comes in only to have a prothrombin time blood test for long-standing use of Coumadin?

Answer: B. Arteries

Explanation: The vessels transport blood and carry way cellular waste and carbon dioxide. The arteries lead away from the heart and branch into arterioles. The veins - lead to the heart and branch into venules. The capillaries connect between arterioles and venules.

V56.6x, Long-term (current) drug use

How many heart chambers are there?
   A. Two
   B. Three
   C. Four
   D. Six

Family history codes are used to show:

Answer: C. Four
Explanation: The two upper chambers are the right atrium and left atrium. The two lower chambers are the right ventricle and the left ventricle.

That a patient has a high risk for contracting a disease, disorder, or condition because a patient has a family member(s) who has or had a particular disease

Which valve lies between the right atrium and the right ventricle?
- A. Aortic
- B. Pulmonary
- C. Tricuspid
- D. Bicuspid

An _____ code is never the first-listed diagnosis.

Answer: C. Tricuspid

Explanation: The tricuspid valve lies between the right atrium and the right ventricle. The pulmonary valve lies between the pulmonary artery and the right ventricle. The aortic valve lies between the aorta and the left ventricle. The bicuspid (mitral) valve lies between the left atrium and the left ventricle.

E

A physician has documented that a blood clot lies in the "epicardial" region. What does this mean?
  A. Under the heart
  B. Over the heart
  C. Beside the heart
  D. Around the heart

A terrorism event resulted in a bus accident. A patient on the bus is brought into the emergency department for a fracture to the right tibia. The physician lists a diagnosis of Fracture to the right tibia, secondary to bus accident. You know to use a code for the terrorism event additionally. In what order would the codes be listed?

Answer: B. Over the heart
Explanation: Epicardial means over the heart.

A first-listed code for the fracture, followed by a secondary code for the terrorism event, and a tertiary code for the bus accident

With the hemolysis process, what substance is broken down?
  A. WBC
  B. Leukocytes
  C. RBC
  D. Plaque

In the ICD-10-CM manual, which codes represent factors that influence health status and contact with health services?

Answer: C. RBC
Explanation: Hemolysis is RBC breakdown.

Z codes

The physician has performed an atherectomy.
What was removed?
- A. Embolism
- B. Blood vessel
- C. Pus
- D. Plaque

With ICD-10-CM, the letter "x" is used as:

Answer: D. Plaque

Explanation: An atherectomy is removal of plaque from an artery, which is done by a percutaneous method. An embolectomy is removal of an embolism or blockage from a vessel. A thoracostomy is a procedure where incisions are made into the chest wall to insert a chest tube, to drain pus. Angioplasty is a procedure used to dilate a vessel opening.

The fifth character dummy placeholder for many 6-character codes.

Which of the following is NOT a risk factor for coronary artery disease (CAD)?
- A. Advancing age
- B. Smoking
- C. Diabetes
- D. Trauma

_____ codes have 3- to 7-digit alphanumeric codes; describe diseases, illnesses, injuries, procedures, and signs/symptoms; and have one or more definitions.

Answer: D. Trauma
Explanation: CAD risk factors include advancing age, family history, hyperlipidemia, hypertension, cigarette smoking, diabetes, and obesity.

ICD-10-CM

Which of the following is another name for a heart attack?

A. Ischemic heart disease
B. Myocardial infarction
C. Hypertension
D. Aneurysm

The ICD-10-CM classification system offers many benefits, such as improved:

Answer: B. Myocardial infarction

Explanation: Coronary artery disease is also called ischemic heart disease. Hypertension is also called high blood pressure. An aneurysm is a dilated blood vessel.

Myocardial infarction (MI) results from myocardial ischemia and is also called a heart attack. The symptoms of this are crushing chest pain and hypotension.

Strategic planning and healthcare delivery system design

All of the following can cause a thrombus EXCEPT:
   A. Infection
   B. Inflammation
   C. Atherosclerosis
   D. Ischemia

True or False: Both ICD-9-CM and ICD-10-CM systems use "unspecified" and "not otherwise specified" codes when a more specific code is not available.

Answer: D. Ischemia
Explanation: A thrombus is also called a blood clot, and it is caused by infection, inflammation, low blood pressure, obstruction, and atherosclerosis.

True

Symptoms of hypotension include:
- A. Dizziness, blurred vision, and syncope
- B. Nosebleeds and cough
- C. Crushing chest pain and irritability
- D. None of the above

True or False: ICD-10-CM uses a dummy placeholder "x" to allow for future expansion and to fill out empty characters when there are less than 6 or when a seventh character applies.

Answer: A. Dizziness, blurred vision, and syncope
Explanation: Hypotension is also called low blood pressure. It is caused by a drop in both systolic and diastolic arterial blood pressure and insufficient oxygen in blood. The symptoms include dizziness, blurred vision, and syncope (fainting).

True

Another name for peripheral artery disease is:
    A. Burger's disease
    B. Buerger's disease
    C. Bogoer's disease
    D. Biguer's disease

What notes in ICD-10-CM advise the coder to look somewhere else before assigning a code?

Answer: B. Buerger's disease
Explanation: Peripheral arterial disease (PAD is also called Buerger's disease. It is inflammation of the peripheral arteries creating vasospasms, which is caused by atherosclerosis.

Cross-reference notes

A group of cardiac diseases that affect the myocardium are:
  A. Arrhythmias
  B. Rheumatic heart diseases
  C. Cardiomyopathies
  D. Valvular diseases

What ICD-10-CM word or phrase means that there is a casual relationship between two conditions?

Answer: C. Cardiomyopathies

Explanation: Cardiomyopathies are a group of cardiac diseases that affect the myocardium. They are caused by idiopathic or existing conditions. Types include dilated cardiomyopathy, hypertrophic cardiomyopathy, and restrictive cardiomyopathy.

Due to

What type of cells has been known to cause an embolism?
   A. Cancer cells
   B. Skin cells
   C. Brain cells
   D. Nerve cells

HCPCS stands for:

Answer: A. Cancer cells

Explanation: An embolism is a mass that enters the bloodstream. Types include air, fat, bacteria, cancer cells, foreign substances, thrombus, and amniotic fluid.

Healthcare Common Procedure Coding System

A patient with varicosities will have what symptoms?
- A. Leg pain and swelling
- B. Leg redness and warmth
- C. Leg vasospasms
- D. Leg cyanosis

Which non-physician services are included in the HCPCS?

Answer: A. Leg pain and swelling
Explanation: Varicose veins are also called varicosities, which occur when blood pools in the veins and distends them. The symptoms include leg swelling, leg pain, leg fatigue, and ulcerations.

Urinary catheter supplies, syringes and needles, and bedside commodes

Which of the following is NOT a cause of infective endocarditis?
- A. Bacteria
- B. Viruses
- C. Fungi
- D. Blood clots

A service related to Temporary Hospital Outpatient Prospective Payment System would be found in which code category?

Answer: D. Blood clots

Explanation: Infective endocarditis is inflammation of the inner lining of the heart that causes permanent heart valve damage. Causes include bacteria, viruses, fungi, or parasites.

C

Which arrhythmia results in rapid, erratic contractions of the heart?
- A. Ventricular fibrillation
- B. Atrial fibrillation
- C. Atrial flutter
- D. Asystole

If a patient has a procedure for an injury to the left upper eyelid, what HCPSC modifier could you use?

Answer: B. Atrial fibrillation

Explanation: Atrial fibrillation (A. fib) is rapid, erratic contractions of the heart. Atrial flutter is rapid regular heart contractions. Ventricular fibrillation is a life-threatening rhythm of random electrical impulses through the ventricles. Asystole is absence of heart rhythm.

–E1

How many types of pericarditis are there?
    A. One
    B. Two
    C. Three
    D. Four

True or False: Low-income children, disabled veterans, and people under the age of 65 are covered by Medicare insurance?

Answer: C. Three

Explanation: Pericarditis is inflammation of the heart pericardium. The types include acute, pericardial effusion, and constrictive.

False. None of these groups are covered by Medicare.

What is the function of the female reproductive external structures?
  A. Enhance sexual stimulation
  B. Protect the body from foreign material
  C. Both A and B
  D. Neither A nor B

Which segment of Medicare covers the Prescription Drug Plan (PDP), which includes Medicare Advantage Plans (MA-PDs), Private Prescription Drug Plans (PDPs), and premiums paid by the beneficiary?

Answer: C. Both A and B

Explanation: The female reproductive system protects the fertilized ovum (egg) for the nine-month gestation period. The external structures enhance sexual stimulation and protect the body from foreign materials. The internal structures produce and release the ovum.

Part D

Which uterine layer is the middle one?
   A. Endometrium
   B. Myometrium
   C. Perimetrium
   D. Vulva

What was the purpose of the National Correct Coding Initiative (NCCI)?

Answer: B. Myometrium

Explanation: The uterus is a muscular organ with three layers: endometrium (inner mucosa), myometrium (middle layer), and perimetrium (outer layer). The vulva is the external genitalia.

To promote national coding methods and control improper coding and reimbursement

The phase of mensuration that spans from day 6 through day 12 is the:
A. Proliferation phase
B. Endometrium repair
C. Secretory phase
D. Premenstruation

What Medicare payment reform established a fee schedule, which allows payment of 80%?

Answer: B. Endometrium repair
Explanation: The phases of menstruation include: the proliferation phase (from day 1 through day 5), the endometrium repair (from day 6 through day 12), the secretory phase (from day 13 through day 14), and premenstruation (from day 15 through day 28).

The Resource-Based Relative Value Scale (RBRVS)

How many days is human gestation?
- A. 166
- B. 236
- C. 266
- D. 336

Current Procedure Terminology (CPT) codes are updated and published by:

Answer: C. 266
Explanation: Human gestation is approximately 9 months or 266 days.

The American Medical Association (AMA)

The third trimester starts at what week of the pregnancy?
   A. Last menstrual period (LMP)
   B. Thirteen
   C. Twenty-eight
   D. Thirty-three

Which codes are used for supplemental tracking and performance measurement?

Answer: C. Twenty-eight
Explanation: Trimesters - First (LMP - 12 weeks), second (13 - 27 weeks), and third (28 weeks - EDD).

Category II codes

The physician has discovered a pregnancy that is "ectopic." What does this mean?
A. Occurred inside the uterus
B. Occurred outside the uterus
C. Termination of pregnancy
D. More than one pregnancy

Level _____ CPT and HCPCS codes contain modifiers, which are 2-digit codes that can be numeric, alphanumeric, and alpha.

Answer: B. Occurred outside the uterus
Explanation: An ectopic pregnancy is one that occurs outside the uterus, usually in the fallopian tube. Termination of pregnancy is abortion, and multipara is more than one pregnancy.

I

A physician documents that there is a lesion at the area between the vagina and anus. What term does this imply?

    A. Cystocele
    B. Antepartum
    C. Introitus
    D. Perineum

Which modifier indicates that the anesthesia services required more time and supplies than usual?

Answer: D. Perineum

Explanation: A cystocele is a herniation of the bladder into the vagina. Antepartum is the time before childbirth. Introitus is the opening of the vagina. The perineum is the region between the vaginal and anus.

-23

A woman is experiencing pelvic cramping at the start of menstruation. What is the medical term to use?

A. Primary dysmenorrhea
B. Secondary dysmenorrhea
C. Primary menorrhagia
D. Secondary menorrhagia

What does modifier -51 indicate?

Answer: A. Primary dysmenorrhea

Explanation: Primary dysmenorrhea is pelvic cramping that occurs at the beginning of menstruation. Secondary dysmenorrhea is painful menstruation due to an underlying condition, such as endometriosis, tumors, or polyps. Menorrhagia is an increase in bleeding amount and duration of flow.

That the same procedure was performed on different sites, that multiple procedures were performed, or that the procedure was performed multiple times

For a condition to be considered primary amenorrhea, which of the following must be true:
  A. Menstruation ceases for 3 cycles.
  B. Menstruation ceases for 6 cycles.
  C. Menstruation ceases for one year.
  D. Menstruation has never occurred.

Which modifier is used when the services need more than one modifier?

Answer: D. Menstruation has never occurred.
Explanation: Primary amenorrhea is a genetic disorder where menstruation has never occurred.

-99

All of the following can cause secondary menstruation EXCEPT:
   A. Stress
   B. Certain foods
   C. Eating disorders
   D. Strenuous exercise

When selecting evaluation and management (E/M) codes, the coder must consider the place of service, type of service, and patient status. What are some possible patient statuses?

Answer: B. Certain foods
Explanation: Secondary amenorrhea is where menstruation ceases for 3 cycles or 6 months. Known causes include stress, tumors, eating disorders, and strenuous exercise.

Inpatient, outpatient, and new patient

Irregular menstrual cycles of varying duration and amounts is called:
A. Metorrhagia
B. Menorrhagia
C. Hypomenorrhea
D. Menometorrhagia

The level of E/M service is based upon:

Answer: D. Menometorrhagia

Explanation: Metorrhagia is bleeding between cycles. Menorrhagia is an increase in bleeding amount and duration of flow. Hypomenorrhea is light or spotty flow.

Effort required, time spent with the patient, and skill necessary to perform the service

Which vaginal infection causes white, curd-like vaginal discharge?
- A. Pelvic inflammatory disease
- B. Gonorrhea
- C. Chlamydia
- D. Candidiasis

What are the three elements of medical decision-making?

Answer: D. Candidiasis
Explanation: Candidiasis, also called a yeast infection, causes white curd-like discharge, pain with sex, and dysuria.

The problem addressed, the data reviewed, and the level of risk

Which of the following is caused by the human papillomavirus?
  A. Pelvic inflammatory disease
  B. Herpes
  C. Condylomata
  D. Gonorrhea

The number of diagnoses and management options is multiple, the risk of death or complications is moderate, and the amount of complexity is also moderate with which type of medical decision-making?

Answer: C. Condylomata

Explanation: Condylomata acuminata (genital warts) is caused by the human papillomavirus. Symptoms include polyps, growths, and warty lesions.

Moderate-complexity

Which condition of pregnancy characterized by edema, hypertension, and proteinuria?
   A. Amenorrhea
   B. Placental previa
   C. Eclampsia
   D. Adenomyosis

Which CPT codes are used for patients not ill enough to be admitted, but those that require monitoring?

Answer: C. Eclampsia

Explanation: Amenorrhea means lack of menstruation. Placenta previa is when the cervical opening is obstructed by placenta. Adenomyosis is an enlarged uterus, abnormal menstrual bleeding, and pain. Eclampsia is the condition of pregnancy characterized by edema, hypertension, and proteinuria.

Hospital Inpatient Services (99221-99239)

A vaginal infection caused by a protozoan is:
- A. Candidiasis
- B. Trichomoniasis
- C. Chlamydia
- D. Gonorrhea

Care Plan Oversight Services (99374-99380) codes are used to report:

Answer: B. Trichomoniasis

Explanation: Candidasis is caused by a fungus. Chlamydia and gonorrhea are both caused by bacteria. Trichomoniasis is caused by the *trichomonas vaginalis* protozoan.

Symptoms include colored vaginal or penis discharge and dysuria.

Physician supervision of patient care in the home health agency setting and physician supervision of patient care in the hospice setting

When a lesion occurs beneath the endometrium, what is the correct term to describe that lesion?
A. Intramural
B. Subserosa
C. Submucous
D. Intermucus

What are some methods of anesthesia?

Answer: C. Submucus

Explanation: Terms include: beneath the endometrium (submucus), beneath the serosa (subserosa), and in the muscle wall (intramural).

Epidural, general, and local

What structure of the male reproduction system produces sperm?

A. Prostate gland
B. Seminal vesicles
C. Bulbourethral gland
D. Testes

The anesthesia formula for payment is:

Answer: D. Testes

Explanation: The testes or gonads produce sperm, as well as testosterone. The prostate gland produces seminal fluid and activates sperm. The seminal vesicles transport sperm from the testes to the exterior. The bulbourethral gland secretes a tiny amount of seminal fluid.

$$(B + T + M) \times \text{Conversion Factor}$$

The structure that lies at the end of the epididymis is:

    A. Prostate gland
    B. Seminal ducts
    C. Vas deferens
    D. Gonads

How many radiology subsections are in the CPT system?

Answer: C. Vas deferens
Explanation: The vas deferens is the tubular structure at the end of the epididymis.

7

What is the surgical procedure to lower undescended testis?
   A. Orchiopexy
   B. Prostatotomy
   C. Vasectomy
   D. TURP

What are the components of the radiology section of CPT?

Answer: A. Orchiopexy

Explanation: Orchiopexy is the surgical procedure to lower undescended testis.

A prostatotomy is an incision to the prostate. Transurethral resection of the prostate (TURP) is a surgical procedure performed by way of cystoscopy to remove some or all of the prostate gland. A vasectomy is removal of a portion of the vas deferens. A vesiculotomy is an incision into the seminal vesicle.

Technical component (TC), professional component, and global component

Which condition can cause severe pain, nausea, vomiting, edema, and fever?
   A. Cryptorchidism
   B. Orchitis
   C. Prostatitis
   D. Testicular torsion

Which radiology codes of CPT are used for various placement of radioactive material into the body, as well as measurement of emissions?

Answer: D. Testicular torsion
Explanation: Testicular torsion is twisting of the testes, which is caused by congenital abnormal development of the tunica vaginalis and spermatic cord or from trauma.
Symptoms include severe pain, nausea, vomiting, edema, and fever.

Nuclear Medicine (78000 - 79999)

Epididymitis is caused from all of the following
EXCEPT:
A. Scrotal pain
B. Trauma
C. Injury
D. Infection

Which CPT codes are used for tests on urine,
blood, breath, feces, and sputum?

Answer: A. Scrotal pain
Explanation: Epididymitis is inflammation of the epididymis. Causes include trauma, injury, or infection. Symptoms include scrotal pain, swelling, redness, and hydrocele.

Chemistry (82000 - 84999)

The two cavities inside the penis are known as the:
A. Epididymis
B. Chordee
C. Corpora cavernosa
D. Varicocele

Cytogenetic Studies (88230 - 88299) CPT codes are used for:

Answer: C. Corpora Cavernosa

Explanation: The epididymis is the structure that holds the sperm, located on the upper portion of the testes. Chordee is a condition where the penis is injured. A varicocele is swelling of a scrotal vein. Corpora cavernosa are the two cavities of the penis.

Collecting, processing, and typing of blood

The physician documents that the urethral meatus is mislocated to the dorsal side of penis. What is this called?

A. Testicular torsion
B. Erispadias
C. Hypospadias
D. Phimosis

Bacteria that cause illness are made nontoxic, and these immunizations are called:

Answer: B. Erispadias

Explanation: A testicular torsion is twisting of the testes. Hypospadias is when the urethral opening occurs on the ventral side of the penis. Phimosis is where the foreskin is constricted and cannot be retracted. Erispadias is where the urethral meatus is mislocated to the dorsal side of penis.

Toxoid

What male reproductive system infection often is caused by E. coli bacteria and causes suprapubic pain, dysuria, and fever?

A. Orchitis
B. Prostatitis
C. Benign prostatic hypertrophy
D. Paraphimosis

Pulmonary (94002 - 94799) CPT codes are used for:

Answer: B. Prostatitis

Explanation: Benign Prostatic Hypertrophy (BPH) is an enlarged prostate gland. Symptoms include nocturia, incontinence, hesitancy, and urinary urgency. Prostatitis is caused by E. coli and other bacteria, and symptoms include fever, low back pain, perineal pain, dysuria, suprapubic tenderness, and UTI.

Ventilation diagnostic tests and ventilation management therapy

What condition is caused by increased levels of hormones and fibrous nodules?
    A. Phimosis
    B. Urethritis
    C. Prostatitis
    D. BPH

Dialysis (90935 - 90999) CPT codes are used for:

Answer: D. BPH
Explanation: BPH is caused by increased levels of hormones and fibrous nodules.
Phimosis is caused by chronic infection or poor hygiene. Urethritis is caused from bacterial organisms, and prostatitis is caused from E.coli and other bacteria.

Hemodialysis

What congenital condition of the penis results in the foreskin constricted and retracted over the penis?

A. Phimosis
B. Paraphimosis
C. BPH
D. Chordee

True or False: Ophthalmology CPT E/M eye codes are used only for eyelid services.

Answer: B. Paraphimosis
Explanation: With phimosis, the foreskin is constricted and cannot be retracted, and this condition is caused by chronic infection and poor hygiene. With paraphimosis, the foreskin is constricted and retracted over the penis.

False

Which of the following is NOT a component of the urinary system?

A. Bladder
B. Ureters
C. Urethra
D. Pancreas

True or False: Allergy and Clinical Immunology (95004 - 95199) CPT codes are used for allergy diagnoses and immunology diagnoses.

Answer: D. Pancreas

Explanation: The urinary system includes the kidneys, ureters, urinary bladder, and urethra. These structures work together to remove metabolic waste materials from the body, such as uric acid, urea, nitrogenous waste, and creatinine. The urinary system also maintains electrolyte balance and assists the liver in body detoxification.

False. Allergy and Clinical Immunology CPT codes are used for neither of these.

What is the outer portion of the kidney called?
   A. Papilla
   B. Hilum
   C. Medullar
   D. Cortex

The biopsy subsection (11100-11101) codes are used for excision of:

Answer: D. Cortex

Explanation: Kidneys are the two organs that control pH balance (acid/base), secrete berenin, vitamin D, and erythropoietin, and stimulate red blood cell production. The cortex is the outer layer of the kidney, the medullar is the inner portion of the kidney, the hilum is the middle section of the kidney, and the papilla is the inner part of the pyramids.

A small piece of skin, a small piece of subcutaneous tissue, and a small piece of mucous membrane tissue

Which procedure involves surgical repair of the urethra?

    A. Cystoplasty

    B. Cystoscopy

    C. Ureterotomy

    D. Urethroplasty

With an incision and drainage code (10400 – 10180), cutting into the skin is considered what?

Answer: D. Urethroplasty

Explanation: Cystoplasty is surgical reconstruction of bladder. Cystoscopy is the use of a scope to view the bladder. Ureterectomy is surgical removal of a ureter. Urethroplasy is the surgical repair of the urethra.

Lancing

All of the following is a type of acute renal failure
EXCEPT:
  A. Interrenal
  B. Intrarenal
  C. Prerenal
  D. Postrenal

You are coding for removal of a benign skin
lesion, using a code from subsection 11400-11646.
What would be included in this procedure?

Answer: A. Interrenal
Explanation: Acute renal failure is the sudden onset of kidney failure. Types include prerenal, intrarenal, and postrenal.

Lesion removal, local anesthesia, and simple closure

Which of the following is NOT a symptom of acute pyelonephritis?
   A. Dysuria
   B. Hypertension
   C. Fever
   D. Nocturia

What type of surgical fracture repair occurs by insertion of devices through the skin or other site?

Answer: B. Hypertension

Explanation: The symptoms of acute pyelonephritis are fever, groin pain, flank pain, dysuria, nausea, pyuria, and nocturia. The symptoms of chronic pyelonephritis are hypertension, dysuria, flank pain, and frequency.

Percutaneous

What kidney infection is caused by Streptococcus?
   A. Cystitis
   B. Acute pyelonephritis
   C. Acute   poststerptococcal
      glomerulonephritis (APSAGN)
   D. Nephrolithiasis

Which CPT surgical procedure codes are used for aspirations, injections, insertions, removals, applications, and adjustments, as well as for various therapeutic sinus tract injections catheter placement, and antibiotics injections?

Answer: C. Acute poststreptococcal glomerulonephritis (APSAGN)

Explanation: Acute poststerptococcal glomerulonephritis (APSAGN) is inflammation of the glomerulus caused by Streptococcus. Symptoms include back pain, flank pain, fatigue, headache, nausea, oliguria, elevated blood pressure, and malaise.

Introduction or Removal (20500-20689)

Of the following kidney conditions, which one is genetic?

A. APSAGN
B. BPH
C. COPD
D. PKD

When are Casting and Strapping (20939-29799) codes NOT used?

Answer: D. PKD

Explanation: APSAGN is caused by Streptococcus. BPH is a condition of the prostate, not the kidney. COPD is a lung condition. Polycystic kidney disease (PKD) is a genetic kidney condition.

When the application of a cast or strap is included in the surgical procedure

Which of the following regulates the gastrointestinal tract?
    A. Local control system
    B. Hormonal system
    C. Neural system
    D. All of the above

The CPT respiratory system subsection includes procedures and services related to the nose, sinuses, larynx, bronchus, trachea, pleura, and lungs, and the codes are divided by:

Answer: D. All of the above

Explanation: The digestive system includes the gastrointestinal tract and various accessory organs. This system functions include absorption, digestion, and elimination. The GI tract is regulated by a complex series of hormonal, neural, and local control systems.

Site, incision, and excision

How many permanent teeth do adults have?
- A. 22
- B. 30
- C. 32
- D. 36

True or False: Diagnostic endoscopy is always included in the surgical endoscopy CPT code.

Answer: C. 32
Explanation: Adults have 32 permanent teeth.

True

Which organ stores bile?
- A. Liver
- B. Gallbladder
- C. Pancreas
- D. Stomach

If the endoscopy procedure begins at the mouth and ends at the bronchial tube, code for:

Answer: B. Gallbladder

Explanation: The stomach is the digestive organ that contains the fundus (upper region), body (middle region), and antrum (lower region). The liver is the digestive organ that produces bile and breaks down wastes. The gallbladder is a small organ that stores bile. The pancreas is the digestive organ that produces enzymes for digestion.

"Bronchial tube = full extent"

What procedure examines the sigmoid colon and rectum via a small scope?
   A. Cholecystectomy
   B. Colonoscopy
   C. Laparoscopy
   D. Proctosigmoidoscopy

The nose incision codes include drain or gauze insertion, as well as removal of lesion or growth. Excision codes in this subsection are intranasal biopsy codes, as well as polyp and turbinate excision and resection. When both sides are involved, use modifier:

Answer: D. Proctosigmoidoscopy

Explanation: Cholecystectomy involves surgical removal of the gallbladder. Colonoscopy is a fiberscopic examination of the colon. Laparoscopy is exploratory procedure of the abdominal cavity using a small scope. Proctosigmoidoscopy is a procedure to examine the sigmoid colon and rectum with a small scope.

-50

What is a hernia?
   A. Tissue or organ protruding through a cavity or the abdominal wall
   B. Protrusion in the wall of the colon
   C. Varicose veins
   D. Artificial opening between the stomach and the abdominal wall

True or False: An electrocardiogram is an example of a noninvasive cardiovascular procedure.

Answer: A. Tissue or organ protruding through a cavity or the abdominal wall

Explanation: A diverticulum is protrusion in the wall of the colon. Varices are varicose veins. A gastrostomy is an artificial opening between the stomach and the abdominal wall.

True

A canker sore is also called a:
- A. Aphthous ulcer
- B. Aphthous stomatitis
- C. Aphthous ulceration
- D. All of the above

Cardiography (93000 - 93278) codes are used for:

Answer: D. All of the above
Explanation: An aphthous ulceration (canker sore, aphthous ulcer, or aphthous stomatitis) is a painful sore on the mouth or lips caused by the herpes simplex virus.

Stress tests, Holter monitors, and electrocardiograms

What infantile condition causes failure to thrive and projectile vomiting?
A. Scleroderma
B. Pyloric stenosis
C. Hiatal hernia
D. Gastritis

What CPT codes are used for various arterial and venous grafting procedures?

Answer: B. Pyloric stenosis

Explanation: Scleroderma does not occur in infants, is atrophy of the lower esophagus smooth muscles, and causes dysphagia esophageal reflex, and strictures. A hiatal hernia occurs in adulthood, is a condition where the diaphragm goes over the stomach, and causes heartburn, belching, reflux, and chest discomfort. Gastritis is an adult condition that results in inflammation of the stomach mucosa, and it causes nausea, vomiting, bleeding, pain, and anorexia.

Venous and Arterial Grafting (33517 - 33536)

Which inflammatory condition causes diarrhea, gas, and abdominal pain, and is associated with aging?

A. Cirrhosis
B. Appendicitis
C. Diverticulitis
D. Pancreatitis

True or False: A radical lymphadenectomy involves removal of aortic and splenic lymph nodes, as well as the surrounding tissue. When this procedure is done along with a major procedure, it should be bundled.

Answer: C. Diverticulitis

Explanation: Cirrhosis is severe liver damage caused by use and liver damage from drugs or viruses, and symptoms are nausea, vomiting, fatigue, jaundice, and edema. Appendicitis is inflammation of the vermiform appendix that projects from the lumen due to infection, and it causes abdominal pain and fever. Pancreatitis is inflammation of the pancreas caused by alcohol, biliary tract obstruction, drug use, gallstones, and viral infections. It produces abdominal pain, fever, septicemia, and general sepsis. Diverticulitis is inflammation of the diverticula in the colon, an aging condition caused by infection with symptoms of diarrhea, gas, and abdominal pain.

True

A small structure of concentrated lymph tissue is called:

- A. Thymus
- B. Tonsil
- C. Lymph node
- D. Spleen

Regarding the hemic and lymphatic systems section, general (38204 - 38242) codes are used for:

Answer: C. Lymph node

Explanation: Lymph sends leaked interstitial fluid into the venous system, assists in immune function, and helps with filtering blood. Lymph nodes are small structures of concentrated lymph tissue. The spleen is a tiny organ located in the left upper abdomen area that filters blood. The thymus is a tiny organ that secretes thymosin and matures the T cells. Tonsils are small tissue structures in the throat.

Bone marrow biopsy, bone marrow harvesting, and bone marrow preservation

Which lymph nodes are located in the armpits?
A. Axillary nodes
B. Jugular nodes
C. Submental nodes
D. Inguinal nodes

Which type of digestive system scope procedure is used to examine and treat the esophagus and past the diaphragm?

Answer: A. Axillary nodes
Explanation: The jugular nodes are located in the neck region, the submental nodes are on the jaw region, and the inguinal nodes are near the groin.

Esophagogastroscopy

Which type of anemia is caused by blood loss, low iron intake, and poor iron absorption?
   A. Aplastic anemia
   B. Iron deficiency anemia
   C. Sickle cell anemia
   D. Hemolytic anemia

Hernia (49491 - 49659) CPT codes are used for various hernia repairs and surgical procedures related to hernias, and they are divided by:

Answer: B. Iron deficiency anemia

Explanation: Aplastic anemia is a group of anemias where bone marrow failure occurs caused by genetics, chemical agents, irradiation, and immunologic factors. Sickle cell anemia involves abnormal sickle-shaped erythrocytes caused by an abnormal type of hemoglobin. Hemolytic anemia is short survival of mature erythrocytes caused by excessive destruction of RBCs.

Type, patient, and presentation

Which disease involves cancer of the blood that occurs more often in children and adolescents and is caused by immature lymphocytes?

   A. CML

   B. CLL

   C. AML

   D. ALL

_____ CPT codes are both unilateral and bilateral.

Answer: D. ALL

Explanation: Chronic Myelogenous Leukemia (CML) is slow, progressive disease that occurs more often in those over 55 caused by mature and immature granulocytes in the bone marrow and blood. Chronic Lymphocytic Leukemia (CLL) is slowly progressive cancer seen more often in older adults caused by increased numbers of mature lymphocytes. Acute Myelogenous Leukemia (AML) is cancer of the blood that has a rapid onset and short survival time that causes fatigue, lymphadenopathy, and bone pain. Acute Lymphocytic Leukemia (ALL) is cancer of the blood that occurs more often in children and adolescents caused by immature lymphocytes.

Kidney (50010 - 50593)

The function of the endocrine system is to:
  A. Produce red blood cells
  B. Regulate thermogenesis
  C. Provide structural support
  D. Manage various body functions by use of hormones

_____ CPT codes are used for transurethral resection of the prostate (TURP) procedures.

Answer: D. Manage various body functions by use of hormones

Explanation: The endocrine system is composed of various glands, as well as ductless endocrine glands that secrete hormones into the blood. This system manages the body by use of chemical messengers called hormones. Other components of this system are pineal gland, hypothalamus, pituitary gland, parathyroid gland, adrenals glands, the pancreas, ovaries, testis, and thymus.

Vesical Neck and Prostate (52400-52700)

Which gland is located at the base of the brain near the sella turica?
 A. Thyroid gland
 B. Parathyroid gland
 C. Pituitary gland
 D. Adrenal gland

_____ CPT codes are used for Cesarean sections.

Answer: C. Pituitary gland

Explanation: The pituitary gland, also called the master gland or hypophysis, is located at the base of the brain near the sella turcica, and it releases numerous hormones. The thyroid gland is located over the trachea, and it secretes thyroxine and triiodothyronine. The parathyroid gland is located on the posterior region of the thyroid gland, and it secretes parathyroid hormone. The adrenal gland is located on top of each kidney, and it secretes corticosteroids (cortisone, aldosterone, and androgens).

Maternity Care and Delivery (59000 - 59899)

Which gland that releases hormones is located above the pituitary gland?
   A. Thymus
   B. Pancreas
   C. Hypothalamus
   D. Pineal gland

Male Genital System (54000 - 55899) destruction codes are divided by:

Answer: Hypothalamus

Explanation: The thymus is located behind the sternum, and it produces thymosin. The pancreas is located behind the stomach, and it secretes insulin and glycogen. The pineal gland is located between the two brain cerebral hemispheres, and it secretes melatonin and neurotransmitters.

Extent of procedure

Which type of diabetes mellitus causes polyuria, polydipsia, and glycosuria?
  A. Type 1
  B. Type 2
  C. Both A and B
  D. Neither A nor B

True or False: Female Genital System (56405 - 58770) destruction codes are divided by extent of procedure and type of procedure.

Answer: Both A and B

Explanation: Diabetes mellitus is a chronic endocrine condition caused by a deficiency in insulin production or poor insulin usage. Both Type I and Type 2 diabetes produce symptoms of polyuria, polydipsia, glycosuria, and weight loss.

False. Female Genital System destruction codes are divided by neither of these.

What causes Cushing's syndrome?
- A. An autoimmune process
- B. Inadequate amounts of thyroid stimulating hormone (TSH) or poor thyroid
- C. Tumors, viruses, autoimmune disorders, infection, and tuberculosis
- D. An overactive adrenal cortex or long-term use of steroids

_____ CPT codes are used for various procedures related to the thyroid, parathyroid, thymus, and adrenal glands.

Answer: D. An overactive adrenal cortex or long-term use of steroids

Explanation: Hyperthyroidism is excess production of thyroid hormone caused by an autoimmune process. Hypothyroidism caused by inadequate amount of thyroid stimulating hormone (TSH) or poor thyroid hormone production. Addison's disease, also called primary adrenal insufficiency is deficiency of adrenocortical hormones caused by tumors, viruses, autoimmune disorders, infection, and tuberculosis. Cushing syndrome, also called hypercortisolism is excessive production of adrenocorticotropic hormone (ACTH) caused by overactive adrenal cortex or long-term use of steroids.

Endocrine System (60000 - 60699)

What are two components of the peripheral
nervous system?
  A. The cranial nerves and the spinal nerves
  B. The brain and the spinal cord
  C. The axon and the myelin sheath
  D. The cerebellum and the cerebrum

The _____ is the outermost skin layer, and it
contains four sections called stratum.

Answer: A. The cranial nerves and the spinal nerves

Explanation: The nervous system controls, regulates, and communicates with the various structures, organs, and body parts. It is made up of the central nervous system (CNS), which is the brain and spinal cord, and the peripheral nervous system (PNS), which involves the cranial and spinal nerves. Neurons are the primary cells of the nervous system. Types include: dendrites (receive nerve signals), cell body (nucleus), axon (carries nerve signals), and mylein sheath (around the axon). The cerebellum and cerebrum are brain structures.

epidermis

How many lumbar vertebrae are there?
- A. 4
- B. 5
- C. 7
- D. 12

The second skin layer is the _____, which contains two sections: the papillary and reticular regions.

Answer: B. 5
Explanation: There are 7 cervical, 12 thoracic, 5 lumbar, 5 sacrum, and 4 coccyx vertebrae.

dermis

Surgical removal of a disc is called:
- A. Craniectomy
- B. Laminectomy
- C. Vertebrectomy
- D. Discectomy

The _____ is subcutaneous tissue, which contains connective tissue and fat tissue. It connects the skin to underlying muscle.

Answer: D. Discectomy

Explanation: Craniectomy is partial, permanent removal of the skull. Laminectomy is surgical excision of the posterior region of the vertebra (spinal process). Vertebrectomy is removal of a vertebra. Discectomy is removal of a vertebral disc.

hypodermis

What reversible condition produces slurred speech, paresthesia of face, and mental confusion?
A. Alzheimer's disease
B. Transient ischemic attack
C. Amyotrophic lateral sclerosis
D. Myasthenia gravis

_____ is fat or fatty tissue.

Answer: B. Transient ischemic attack

Explanation: Transient ischemic attack (TIA) is temporary reduction of blood flow to the brain causes stroke-like symptoms caused by cerebrovascular disease. It produces slurred speech, paresthesia of face, and mental confusion short term.

Adipose

Which sense is associated with cranial nerve one (CN1)?
    A. Touch
    B. Sight
    C. Smell
    D. Hearing

A _____ is the removal of a small section of tissue.

Answer: C. Smell
Explanation: Olfactory sense receptors are located in the nasal cavity and associated with Cranial Nerve I (CNI).

biopsy

Fluid in front of the lens is called:
A. Sclera
B. Vitreous humor
C. Aqueous humor
D. Choroid

_____ is a localized collection of blood.

Answer: C. Aqueous humor

Explanation: The sclera is the white of the eye that extends from the cornea to the optic nerve. The choroid is the middle layer of the eye that contains pigment. The retina is the inner layer of the eye that contains rods and cones. The aqueous humor is fluid in front of the lens, whereas the vitreous humor is fluid behind the lens.

Hematoma

Which of the following is also called the eardrum?
  A. Ossicle
  B. Stapes
  C. Auricle
  D. Tympanic membrane

_____ is a malignant tumor of the skin.

Answer: D. Tympanic membrane
Explanation: Ossicles are the small inner ear bones, which include the malleus, incus, and stapes. The auricle, also called the pinna, is the structure that allows sound waves to enter the ear. The tympanic membrane is the inner ear eardrum.

Melanoma

What is ptosis?
  A. Drooping of the upper eyelid
  B. Blocked nasolacrimal duct
  C. Eyelid inflammation
  D. Nearsightedness

_____ tissue is heart muscle that is both striated and smooth.

Answer: A. Drooping of the upper eyelid
Explanation: Dacryocystitis is a blocked nasolacrimal duct, blepharitis is eyelid inflammation, and myopia is nearsightedness.

Cardiac

A physician documents that he created a small opening in the middle ear. What is this called?
   A. Apicectomy
   B. Mastoidectomy
   C. Keratoplasty
   D. Fenestration

_____ tissue is striated tissue that attaches to bones.

Answer: D. Fenestration

Explanation: An apicectomy is removal of a portion of the temporal bone. A mastoidectomy is removal of the mastoid bone. Keratoplasty is surgical repair of the cornea. Fenestration is the creation of a small opening in the middle ear.

Skeletal

Macular degeneration is:
  A. Destruction of the fovea centralis
  B. Age-related
  C. Loss of central vision
  D. All of the above

_____ tissue is smooth tissue that lines the bowel, blood vessels, and urethra.

Answer: D. All of the above
Explanation: Macular degeneration is destruction of the fovea centralis that occurs with age. The main symptom is loss of central vision.

Visceral

CPSIA information can be obtained
at www.ICGtesting.com
Printed in the USA
FFHW012104190219
50614565-55983FF